Take a trip to

CENTRAL AMERICA

Keith Lye

General Editor

Henry Pluckrose

Franklin Watts

London New York Sydney Toronto

Facts about Central America

Belize
Area: 22,965 sq. km.
(8,867 sq. miles)
Population: 186,000
Capital: Belmopan
(pop. 4,000)

Costa Rica
Area: 50,700 sq. km.
(19,575 sq. miles)
Population: 2,495,000
Capital: San José
(pop. 272,000)

El Salvador
Area: 21,041 sq. km.
(8,124 sq. miles)
Population: 5,494,000
Capital: San Salvador
(pop. 430,000)

Guatemala
Area: 108,889 sq. km.
(42,042 sq. miles)
Population: 8,413,000
Capital: Guatamala City
(pop. 1,300,000)

Honduras
Area: 112,088 sq. km.
(43,277 sq. miles)
Population: 4,398,000
Capital: Tegucigalpa
(pop. 533,000)

Nicaragua
Area: 130,000 sq. km.
(50,193 sq. miles)
Population: 3,320,000
Capital: Managua
(pop. 820,000)

Panama
Area: 77,082 sq. km.
(29,762 sq. miles)
Population: 2,226,000
Capital: Panama City
(pop. 467,000)

ISBN: UK Edition 0 86313 273 1
ISBN: US Edition 0 531 10010 3
Library of Congress Catalog
Card No: 85-50162

© Franklin Watts Limited 1985

Printed in Hong Kong

Maps: Tony Payne
Design: Edward Kinsey
Stamps: Stanley Gibbons Limited
Photographs: Zefa; Paul Forrester 10;
Robert Harding, 15, 23, 31; J. Allan
Cash, 25, 26; Camerapix Hutchison, 27
Front cover: Zefa
Back cover: J. Allan Cash

Central America is a land bridge
joining North and South America. It
contains seven countries and cuts off
the Caribbean Sea from the Pacific
Ocean. The first people to live here
were American Indians. Today,
many people are of mixed Indian and
European origin, called mestizos.

One group of American Indians, the Mayans, founded a great civilization in Central America. It reached the height of its power between AD 300 and 900. These Mayan ruins are at Tikal, in northern Guatemala.

The Mayan empire stretched from Mexico to Honduras. This ancient Mayan altar is at Copán, in Honduras. Here, the Mayans made sacrifices to their gods. The Mayans were great mathematicians.

Spanish ships explored the eastern coasts of Central America from 1501. By 1525, Spanish soldiers had seized the entire area. They introduced Christianity. More than nine out of every ten people are now Roman Catholics. This church is in Panama.

Antigua was the capital of Guatemala until it was nearly destroyed by an earthquake in 1773. A new capital was founded at Guatemala City. The picture shows a church and a palace, which once housed Spanish officers.

Some Blacks live in Central America. They are the descendants of African slaves. This girl lives in Belize. Britain ruled Belize from 1862 to 1981. Its official language is English. Spanish is used in the other countries.

Guatemala City, capital of Guatemala, is Central America's largest city and the only one with more than a million people. Guatemala became independent from Spain in 1821, together with the other Spanish territories.

The picture shows some of the stamps used in the Central American countries. Some of them show the beautiful birds found in the forests.

10

WORLD
MAP

Central America

MEXICO

Tikal •
Belize
•Belmopan

Guatemala

•San Pedro Sula

Honduras

CARIBBEAN
SEA

Guatemala City•

San Salvador•
El Salvador

•Tegucigalpa

CENTRAL AMERICA

Nicaragua

Managua•

Lake Nicaragua

Costa Rica

PACIFIC
OCEAN

San José•

Panama Canal

•Colón
•Panama

COLOMBIA

Panama

11

San José, capital of Costa Rica, is the region's fourth largest city. Costa Rica and the other Spanish-speaking countries are republics. But Belize's Head of State is the British monarch, with a Governor-General in Belize.

San Salvador is the capital of El Salvador, Central America's smallest country. El Salvador and Honduras are the poorest countries in this underdeveloped region. About 44 out of every 100 people in Central America now live in cities and towns.

Central America has many cone-shaped volcanoes. Some are extinct, but others are active. The highest peak in Central America is a volcano called Volcán Tajumulco, in Guatemala. It is 4,220 m (13,845 ft) high.

Earthquakes and volcanic eruptions cause great destruction in Central America. The picture shows earthquake damage in Managua, Nicaragua, in 1972. In 1976, an earthquake in Guatemala caused the deaths of 24,000 people.

Central America is a tropical region with high temperatures and heavy rain, especially on the coastal plains. The highlands are cooler. Forests cover many areas. The villages are in forest clearings, as here in Costa Rica.

Nicaragua, the largest country in Central America, contains its largest lake, Lake Nicaragua. This lake has an area of about 7,700 sq km (3,000 sq miles). It has plenty of fish. A volcanic island lies in the lake.

Farming employs about 50 out of every 100 Central Americans, as compared with 20 who work in industry. Much of the farmland is devoted to maize, the chief food crop. This maize-producing farm is in Guatemala.

The most valuable crop in the highlands of Central America is coffee. This picture was taken in Costa Rica which, with Guatemala, El Salvador, Honduras and Nicaragua, is among the world's top 20 coffee producers.

Honduras ranks ninth in the world in producing bananas and bananas are this country's main export. Costa Rica, Panama and Guatemala are also major producers of bananas, which grow well on the hot, wet coastal plains.

Fishing provides a useful source of food in Central America. This fishing port is on Roatán, the largest of the Bay Islands in the Caribbean Sea belonging to Honduras. Lobsters and shrimps are caught here.

The Panama Canal is an 82 km
(51 mile) long waterway. It links the
Caribbean Sea to the Pacific Ocean.
It is a short cut for ships. It was built
by American engineers in 1904–1914.
The canal is now controlled by an
American and Panamanian board.

The Panama Canal is one of the world's greatest engineering wonders. Ships have to pass through a series of locks (water-filled chambers), where they are raised or lowered from one level to another. The picture shows the Miraflores Locks.

Most Central American children enjoy school. They know that educated people usually have higher standards of living than uneducated ones. In Panama, education is free and compulsory for children aged 7 to 15 years.

This village school is in Costa Rica, which has free primary and secondary school education. Costa Ricans are among the best educated people in Central America. Nearly all the adults can read and write.

Most Central American families are large. In country areas, the women and children usually help the men in working on the family farm. On market days and religious festivals, they all wear their best clothes.

More and more people are moving to the cities. They hope to get jobs and enjoy the services which cities offer. But jobs and houses are often in short supply. Many people have to live in slums, as here in Managua, Nicaragua.

Farmers in Guatemala try to
produce a little more food than they
need to feed their families. The
surplus food is sold and the money is
used to buy such necessary items as
clothes and medicines for the
children.

Central America has a good road network, although travel is sometimes difficult in the mountains. The buses are often crowded and weighed down by luggage piled high on the roof. This picture was taken in Guatemala.

In parts of Guatemala, some people still follow the old Mayan religion. Others combine the old beliefs with Christianity. But the vast majority of the people are Roman Catholics.

Central America is changing quickly. Modern technology and industry contrast with the simple lifestyles of the peasant farmers, which have stayed more or less the same for hundreds of years. This picture shows old and new forms of transportation in Belize.

Index